Twenty Days In Colossians

Set Your Mind On
THINGS ABOVE

Brief commentary by Warren Berkley
"Another Look" by Randy Harshbarger

2025: One Stone Press.
All rights reserved. No part of this book may be reproduced in any form without written permission of the publisher.

Published by:
One Stone Press
979 Lovers Lane
Bowling Green, KY 42103

Printed in the United States of America

ISBN 978-1-966992-03-5

"Scripture quotations are from the ESV® Bible (The Holy Bible, English Standard Version®), © 2001 by Crossway, a publishing ministry of Good News Publishers. Used by permission. All rights reserved. The ESV text may not be quoted in any publication made available to the public by a Creative Commons license. The ESV may not be translated in whole or in part into any other language."

"Scripture quotations taken from the (NASB®) New American Standard Bible®, Copyright © 1960, 1971, 1977, 1995, 2020 by The Lockman Foundation. Used by permission. All rights reserved. lockman.org "

1(800)428-0121 • www.onestone.com

Dedication

Paula Berkley Dunn

November 12, 1952—September 7, 2024

Foreword

In his delightful little study of the book of Colossians, *The All-Sufficient Christ*, William Barclay warned that "We are seldom quite free from the danger of forgetting that Jesus said, 'Follow Me,' not, 'Discuss Me.'"[1]

Barclay's caution points to a major problem that plagues our modern conception of Christianity. For too many people, Jesus is a topic of discussion rather than emulation. He is treated as the "founding father" of a great bureaucratic institution that is free to chart its own path through history; or as the figurehead of a rich philosophical system— an exemplary teacher, no doubt, but otherwise uninvolved. He has been reduced to a topic for lively discussion that stirs the intellectual juices but otherwise remains impotent as an instrument of personal transformation.

No part of the New Testament challenges these distortions of Jesus' place in the cosmos more effectively than Paul's epistle to the Colossians. Its message of "the all-sufficient Christ" (to borrow Barclay's label) is an essential corrective to the detours that relegate Jesus to a mere discussion topic. If we could grasp Paul's message in this little book, it would revolutionize our religion, our thoughts, and our lives.

In this study guide, Warren Berkley echoes Barclay's warning: "The gospel is not a message that Christ is just a part of. Christ is at the center of the message" (p. 20). Until we recognize Jesus Christ as the Lord of our lives—indeed, of all the universe—His power to transform us is weakened, no matter how much we might talk about Him. If we really grasped its significance, this "good news" about what Jesus has accomplished and the position He now occupies would radically alter every aspect of our being.

Warren Berkley has been a personal friend for almost half a century. From the beginning of our relationship, his studious treatment of the Word and his ability to articulate its message has stood out from the crowd. Those qualities shine in this treatment of the Colossian letter. Warren places the sacred text front and center in each daily study session. His comments on the text draw our attention to the apostle's message, rather than human speculation. More importantly, he high-

---

[1] *The All-Sufficient Christ: Studies in Paul's Letter to the Colossians*, Westminster Press, 1963, p. 135.

lights Paul's message of the supremacy of Christ in all things, restoring Him to His rightful place at the center of our lives.

Only by plumbing the depths of the divine mystery, "which is Christ in you, the hope of glory" (Col. 1:27), will we benefit from its beauty. My prayer is that this study guide will not only spark fruitful discussions about Jesus but also inspire students to get serious about what it means to follow Him in every aspect of their lives.

David King

DAY 1

Read: Colossians 1:1,2

Colossae was a city in a region called Asia Minor. If you were to visit that physical location today, you would be in modern Turkey.

A main road led from Ephesus over toward the East and the Euphrates Valley. Colossae was on that route. Another geographic marker is this city rested on the banks of the Lycus River. Other cities in the area were Laodicea and Hierapolis.

Colossae was like a health resort to many tourists, well known for its abundant supply of medicinal waters and natural baths (similar to places like Hot Springs, Arkansas or comparable places in Colorado or Oregon).

Concerning the church at Colossae, we do not have specific background information. When we study Philippians, Ephesians, Thessalonians, and the letter to Corinth – we can refer back to the book of Acts and discover the history of when those churches were first formed. We do not have the specific history to inform us of how this church came into existence.

There might be some inferential conclusions. There was extensive preaching in the region of Asia Minor (we can follow that work in Acts 16, 18, 19, and 20). From those passages, we conclude the gospel was taken into this region, people obeyed the gospel, shared the gospel, and local churches came into existence as Christians assembled and worked together. Along with this, there is the reality of individual devotion to spreading the gospel. As people traveled or conversed with travelers, they delivered the message. This "chain-reaction" process took the gospel to places where Christ had not yet been preached. {Today, we call this "personal evangelism." Yet, using that terminology doesn't spread the gospel. Becoming energetically engaged in personal evangelism is compulsory.}

There is something some call *The Philemon Connection* (see Col. 4:7-9). The name Onesimus is there. He was the slave who returned to Philemon, and that story is told in Philemon. All considered, it is highly possible that Philemon and Onesimus were members of this church in Colossae. Along with this, there is the probability the church met in the home of Philemon.

The writer of Colossians was the Apostle Paul, and he was accompanied by Timothy when he wrote this letter to the Christians in Colossae.

There was a problem in Colossae, a threat Paul needed to deal with. Like Ezra, Nehemiah, and the prophets, when God's people see a threat, the faithful reaction of teaching and admonition follows.

There was a system of religious error that was insidious and pervasive in the area. It was a movement or system that wasn't in keeping with the truth of Christ the apostles revealed. It was a religious system created by men, not God. Some in Colossae were enamored with this new thing. In chapter two, Paul addressed this with genuine apostolic authority, love for the truth based on love for God, and love for souls.

This religious error was a blend, a mixture of religion and philosophy and carnal distortions. Since it was gaining popularity, Paul needed to hit this with the truth to keep people alert and spiritually safe. Dealing with religious error is another illustration of the good fight of faith (1 Tim. 6:12) and the defense and confirmation of the gospel (Phil. 1:7).

The Colossian Heresy seems to have been a corrupt combination or blend of Judaism, Gnosticism, Paganism, and Materialism (very similar to modern-day New Age religion).

From this epistle, we can learn the gospel is not available to be mixed or married to anything man invents, whether it be one man or a group.

Therefore, a dominant theme in Colossians is the preeminence of Jesus Christ and faithful devotion to His message, the gospel. When we become His followers, we surrender our lives to Him, who died for us. The authority He has over us is not to be shared with another. We cannot connect or mix the truths of the gospel with the philosophies of men. Before Paul gets into all this, he says to his brethren:

> [1] *Paul, an apostle of Christ Jesus by the will of God, and Timothy our brother,* [2] *To the saints and faithful brothers in Christ at Colossae: Grace to you and peace from God our Father (Colossians 1:1-2 ESV).*

ANOTHER LOOK!

LIVING IN COLOSSAE

"Paul, an apostle of Jesus Christ by the will of God, and Timothy our brother, To the saints and faithful brethren in Christ who are at Colossae: Grace to you and peace from God our Father" Colossians 1:1-2 NASB 95). Living in the city of Colossae would not be easy. Located on a major east-to-west trade route, the city was a conduit for wealth and prosperity. Paul's warning about covetousness was appropriate (Colossians 3:5). Colossae was laced with temples honoring Artemis, Zeus, and Isis. This paganism meant that God's people would have to stand against prevailing popular beliefs and attitudes and, at the same time, maintain their own personal standards of purity—stand against something, but, yes, stand for something! Gnosticism, Judaism, Asceticism, and will-worship point to nuanced, idiosyncratic teachings that denied the supremacy and sufficiency of Jesus Christ. Any discussion, explanation, or application of Colossians must never stray from these two prevailing themes. Paul says: Wake up! Be alert! "See to it that no one takes you captive through philosophy and empty deception, according to the tradition of men, according to the elementary principles of the world, rather than according to Christ" (Colossians 2:8 NASB 95). Don't forget—Christ is enough!

What did God's people in Colossae have that would help them truly be the church that belonged to Christ? They had what Paul had: the interest and goodwill of God the Father. Arguably a great man, Paul would only say that he was what he was by God's grace (1 Corinthians 15:10). Accordingly, he offered a committed heart to the Lord. If the saints in Colossae were on the verge of wavering, Paul encourages them. His salutation was not perfunctory. He says remember Jesus Christ and acknowledge the will of God. Timothy is pulling for you, too. You have each other. You are in Christ! If the Colossians were to grow in faith and persevere against false teaching, they would need grace and peace from God. That is what Paul was praying about. Will we join him in prayer?

Randy Harshbarger

DAY 2

Read: Colossians 1:3-8

From the time of Paul's conversion to the Lord, he was "always" thankful to God and always encouraged his brothers and sisters to be thankful (see also Philippians chapter 1). Through his hardships, disappointments, and all the persecution he suffered, he maintained a firm grasp on gratitude. *There is never a time to turn loose of gratitude!*

It wasn't, for Paul, a routinely worded prayer three times a day with meals. Embedded in Paul's character was this strong presence of gratitude to God for his salvation, his opportunities, his heavenly future, and his God-given abilities to tell the good news of Christ. He and the others, like Peter, were devoted to speaking the oracles of God: "*Whoever speaks, as one who speaks oracles of God,*" (1 Pet. 4:11).

Another strong element of Paul's character was his prayers for his brethren. He prayed for every Christian he knew, if not by specific name or group, there was an inclusive scope in praying for all Christians universally, always giving glory to God for the good people who followed Christ.

Paul "heard of" the faith and love of the saints in Colossae. And, he knew their faith and love were produced by "the hope laid up" for them "in heaven." (They heard about all this when they listened to gospel preaching!)

To the Colossians and to "the whole world," the gospel had been preached before Paul wrote this letter and the proclamation continued. Not only had the gospel been preached, it was "bearing fruit and growing." (Are we continuing to preach the gospel to the lost? If not, what's wrong, and how do we react to our neglect?)

This is what the gospel does! It conveys the hope of heaven and the promise of forgiveness. When hearers believe, repent, and obey, their lives bear fruit. This enables them and others to appreciate "the grace of God in truth."

The Colossian Christians had learned the gospel through the good work of Epaphras, a fellow servant with Paul. Of him, Paul said, "He is a faithful minister of Christ on your behalf." (See also 4:12 and Philemon 1:23.)

Verse 8: "And has made known to us your love in the Spirit." Epaphras delivered the gospel to Colossae and reported the good results to Paul - specifically, their love in the Spirit. Their love in the Spirit was a love for truth, love for the divine originator of truth, and love to be obedient to the truth, as revealed by the Holy Spirit.

This text reminds us of how the gospel enlightens and changes people. This reality should prompt us to preach the gospel and be permanently thankful to God for His grace and those who serve Him.

From the Christian Standard Bible:

> *3 We always thank God, the Father of our Lord Jesus Christ, when we pray for you, 4 for we have heard of your faith in Christ Jesus and of the love you have for all the saints 5 because of the hope reserved for you in heaven. You have already heard about this hope in the word of truth, the gospel 6 that has come to you. It is bearing fruit and growing all over the world, just as it has among you since the day you heard it and came to truly appreciate God's grace. 7 You learned this from Epaphras, our dearly loved fellow servant. He is a faithful minister of Christ on your behalf, 8 and he has told us about your love in the Spirit.*

ANOTHER LOOK!

SHOWING APPRECIATION

Showing appreciation for others is a good thing. Even though Paul was in prison, he still recognized and affirmed the faith, hope, and love of the Christians in Colossae (Colossians 1:3-5). The recognition of something positive in someone can lead to greater good and greater activity. Paul was confident the Colossians would continue bearing fruit for the Lord. It is difficult to understand the daily pressures these early Christians lived with. Colossae's large Jewish population, thanks in part to the relocation schemes of Antiochus Epiphanes decades earlier, meant that the lure of Judaism was strong. Paul says: Do not be deceived by the shadow; have faith in Christ, the reality. Spiritual completeness was possible; Paul's interest in these folks would spur them to greater victories for the Lord.

We must not overlook the power of the gospel. Colossae's smorgasbord of philosophies was well-supplied. If Gnosticism was a real threat to the Colossians (is it better to say insipient Gnosticism?), then these Christians needed to hold to the truth. Whether full-blown or not, easily identified or not (the so-called Colossian Heresy), Paul attacks all efforts to undermine the completeness Christ provides. "For it was the Father's good pleasure for all the fullness to dwell in Him" (Colossians 1:19 NASB 95). Angels and gods do not rule. Eating certain foods or not eating, abusing the body, or neglecting the body—all efforts to supplement Christ fail. "These are matters which have, to be sure, the appearance of wisdom in self-made religion and self-abasement and severe treatment of the body but are of no value against fleshly indulgence" (Colossians 2:23 NASB 95).

The Golden Era of Greek philosophy has passed. Still, there are many things that remain true; there are many things that only appear to be true. The devil can quote scripture; he also tells lies. Mankind continues that infinite search for a grounding, a tent peg, an anchor to avert the aimless drifting of life. Let's be thankful for each other—for those who have mutual faith, hope, and love. The first Adam believed what the devil said. Let us believe what the last Adam is saying to us.

Randy Harshbarger

14

DAY 3

Read: Colossians 1:9-14

THE APOSTLE PAUL NOT ONLY TAUGHT PEOPLE THE TRUTH, BUT HE PRAYED THAT THEY WOULD RECEIVE IT, REMEMBER IT, USE IT, AND BE STRENGTHENED BY IT.

There was this genuine affection for those who heard him preach and teach or read his letters. The most effective teaching and preaching is done by those who have genuine affection for people. Throughout Paul's epistles, this love for people is apparent. He loved God, Christ, the Holy Spirit, and the message he delivered. This love was not a wavering, immature, easily broken emotion. It was real because his relationship with God was real.

But it wasn't just that Paul wanted the Colossian Christians to hear, learn, and know. Another dimension of his love for God and God's people was He wanted them to "walk in a manner worthy of the Lord, fully pleasing to Him, bearing fruit in every good work and increasing in the knowledge of God."

Just hearing, reading, remembering, knowing, and teaching are not sufficient. All that reception of knowledge must result in actually walking—living "in a manner worthy of the Lord."

The intention of every individual Christian must be to "fully please" the Lord, "bearing fruit in every good work," and "increasing in the knowledge of God."

This was Paul's prayer for these Christians "from the day" he heard of their existence. Following that day, he prayed without ceasing for them. He prayed for them to be strong, "strengthened with all power, according to His glorious might," so they could endure difficulty with patience and joy, giving thanks to the Father. It was God, the Father, who enabled them to have this knowledge. And, the Father qualified the Colossian Christians "to share in the inheritance of the saints in light." God does the qualifying. His will is the means of this inheritance, and His grace makes light available to those who desire to be saints. We become recipients of

His grace when we accept "the inheritance of the saints in light" and walk in that light. Baptism is when we leave darkness and step into the light.

We submit to His will in baptism and faithfulness. Christians can say and sing to one another these words: "He has delivered us from the dominion of darkness and transferred us to the kingdom of His beloved son, in whom we have redemption, the forgiveness of sins."

Think of this as (1) being delivered and (2) being transferred. When someone hears, believes, and obeys the gospel (confession, repentance, and baptism), God delivers that person from the darkness of sin and places that person in His kingdom of light. It is an inheritance of light and grace (for people who came out of darkness and do not deserve such consideration.).

Thanks be to God for all this. In Christ, "we have redemption, the forgiveness of sins."

ANOTHER LOOK!

KNOWLEDGE OF GOD

"So that you will walk in a manner worthy of the Lord, to please Him in all respects, bearing fruit in every good work and increasing in the knowledge of God" (Colossians 1:10 NASB 95). When Paul speaks about the knowledge of God, does he mean knowledge about God, or does he refer to the knowledge that God gives, knowledge in this case, given through the Bible? The fact that God IS means there must be certain knowledge about Him. If someone or something did not exist, there would be nothing to know. Great thinkers (Bacon, Aristotle, Kant) spoke of theoretical, moral, and productive knowledge. "Most philosophers therefore agree that knowledge requires a true belief that is justified or warranted or that has been acquired through a reliable process, though there is great disagreement as to what it is that warrants or justifies a belief" (*Pocket Dictionary of Apologetics and Philosophy of Religion*, Evans, 66). There are arguments in Colossians about what is true, what needs to be in tune with the Lord, and what kind of knowledge is truly wise and valuable.

We must have knowledge to live truly for the Lord. Head knowledge is good; we must go beyond in our application of what we know to be true. There is something to know about God; there is something to believe and to act on. That is what Paul calls "working out our salvation." Some do not know the truth. Some know the truth and reject it. Some know the truth and disdain it. Some know the truth and cherish it fervently. We should be thankful that we know anything at all about God. We know so little, but we can know more. We can learn about God; His will reveals who He is and who we should be. And if we get sidetracked by false knowledge, do not forget to look to Jesus. "No one has seen God at any time; the only begotten God who is in the bosom of the Father, He has explained Him" (John 1:18).

Randy Harshbarger

DAY 4

Read: Colossians 1:15-20

If you are a Christian, this is what you believe about Jesus Christ. These truths are non-negotiable premises upon which your confidence in Christ rests.

He is the image of the invisible God. All that God is shows up perfectly in the person and work of Jesus Christ. (See also Hebrews 1:3)

The firstborn is not a reference to sequence. It doesn't mean Jesus was the first one born (see Joh. 1:1-3 & Col. 1:16,17). The term, as used here, is about rank. Jesus stands above all creation, and the phrase is so rendered in the New King James and New International Version. This is an affirmation of the superiority of Jesus Christ above all.

In harmony with this, "By Him all things were created, in heaven and on earth, visible and invisible, whether thrones or dominions or rulers or authorities – all things were created through Him and for Him." It is entirely appropriate to call Jesus the Creator. He was not only there; He was active in the work of creation (see also Joh. 1:1-3). Nothing is left out in Paul's statement. Jesus was involved in the total work of divine creation in the beginning.

Therefore, "...He is before all things, and in Him all things hold together." The work of Jesus as Creator continues now in His ongoing work of sustaining and holding together what He made. He keeps this universe running.

In keeping with all these truths about Him, "He is the head of the body, the church. He is the beginning, the firstborn from the dead, that in everything he might be preeminent." If you have been baptized into the body of Christ, you now live under the Head as a member of His body, subservient to Him. "In everything," He should be preeminent in your life (see also Col. 3:17). This is not merely an obligation, in some sort of dry or routine sense. This describes our attachment, our dependence, and, by extension, our gratitude that we have perfect guidance.

Verse 19 is a critical part of this paragraph that affirms the truth about the person and work of Jesus Christ: "For in Him all the fullness of God was pleased to dwell." Jesus was not a half-god or part-god. This is a statement of His full deity. He was never and can never be less than God. (Phil. 2:7 does not contradict this. While He left heaven and lived in a human body, Col. 2:9 states that in Him, all the fullness of deity "dwells bodily.")

All of the above is important because our problem is sin. God acted with Jesus Christ and the Holy Spirit to provide a solution to our problem (see also 1 Pet. 1:1-3). Through Christ, God is willing to reconcile those who want to come out of sin. "And through Him to reconcile to Himself all things, whether on earth or in heaven, making peace by the blood of His cross."

Do you see what Paul does? He affirms the truth about the person and work of Jesus Christ – and takes that truth to God's gracious offer to reconcile us to Him, "making peace by the blood of His cross."

This is what we believe. All our thinking, speaking, and living are based on who Jesus is and what He did for us. Be obedient. Be Thankful.

Teaching this passage a few years ago, to emphasize this point I said:

> *The Islamic religion does not provide reconciliation with God. The Roman Catholic system does not provide reconciliation with God. Denominational creeds do not provide reconciliation with God. The New Age Gnostic philosophy (even when mixed with biblical terms) does not reconcile sinners to God.*

There is only one way to get out of sin, escape from its consequences, cancel the guilt, and enter into fellowship with God. It is through Jesus Christ and "the blood of His cross."

ANOTHER LOOK!

APOLOGISTS FOR CHRIST

"For it was the Father's good pleasure for all the fullness to dwell in Him" (Colossians 1:19 NASB 95). If Jesus is before all things and if all things in Jesus consist, then there is no room for another savior regardless of how wise or powerful the usurper claims to be. There are no cracks in the door; all loopholes are closed. Christ, our Creator, brings redemption. He sustains us spiritually; our world continues because of His active power. The thrones and principalities of Paul's time needed to pay attention. Christ's victory on the cross dealt a death blow to those who claimed He was not enough. He might be useful, yes, but without the worship of angels, without the use and misuse of the body, and along with esoteric slogans, the enemies of the cross said one could not advance spiritually. Really? Paul said. "When He had disarmed the rulers and authorities, He made a public display of them, having triumphed over them through Him" (Colossians 2:15).

In the second century AD, there was a group of men known as "Christian Apologists." At a time when demands for Caesar worship were increasing, they wrote in defense of Christianity. It may seem odd, but these Apologists wrote about "atheism, cannibalism, and incest." Atheists refused to follow the crowd and observe certain rituals and ceremonies. The fact that Christians believed in God was not enough. The charge of cannibalism stemmed from these early Christians partaking of the Lord's Supper. It is easier to see at least some connection between this charge and the body and blood of Jesus; the charge was false, of course, but Christians were often called to account for their misunderstood practices. Some Gnostics claimed to be Christians. Their libertine practices regarding physical, fleshly activities (immorality) were imputed to all the other Christians, who became guilty by association (*Church History*, Vol. 1, Ferguson, 66-67). Irenaeus wrote against the Gnostics in his *Against Heresies*. A more recent writer, Elaine Pagels, extols the value of Gnosticism in her book, *The Gnostic Gospels. The Gospel of Thomas*, part of the Nag Hammadi scrolls, discovered in 1945, is integral to her thesis that Gnostic Christianity comes as close as anything to true New Testament Christianity, at least as close as anything that has been discovered to this point in time.

What kind of God do we want? Do we want a therapeutic God who makes us feel good when we are sad, when our feelings get hurt, or when someone ignores us? Any attempt to redefine who Jesus is amounts to efforts to make God in our image. Paul says that Jesus is the firstborn of creation; He is of first rank and importance. Jesus was not (is not) a created being; He is God; there has never been a time when Jesus did not exist. He is the image, the exact representation and revelation of God. If Greek philosophy is true, namely, that in the world, there is a primary cause, an instrumental cause, and a final cause, then we need look no further than Jesus. Jesus is the cause, the planner, the instrumentality, the producer. He is complete. And guess what? He loves us!

Randy Harshbarger

DAY 5

Read: Colossians 1:21-29

It is hard for most of us to understand *rejoicing while suffering*.

Typically, we "cope" with suffering by complaining, blaming, or feigning (acting like we are OK). Paul's attitude should cause us to pause and re-examine the sturdiness of our faith. Paul said to his brothers and sisters in Colossae: "Now, I rejoice in my sufferings." First, he knew his suffering was temporary (see 2 Cor. 4:17). Second, he submitted to suffering without typical complaining *for the sake of the needs of Christians!* Third, part of his purpose was to illustrate to others how joy and suffering are combined.

It is right in verse 24: "Now I rejoice in my sufferings for your sake." For their sake – that is, for the sake of their knowledge and edification, Paul kept suffering with unselfish endurance. He wanted his light to shine in their presence. (Consider how utterly discouraging it would be for Christians in Colossae to witness Paul folding up or hiding under pressure.)

Fourth, the apostle saw his suffering from this high perspective: "I am filling up what is lacking in Christ's afflictions for the sake of His body, that is, the church."

This cannot mean that anything about Christ's suffering and death was lacking. While the translation may be awkward, the only way to understand this (compatible with everything else the New Testament says about the perfect sacrifice of Christ)—is that Paul, no matter how much he suffered, would always be "lacking." He would spend his life "filling up" what was lacking in his suffering; his fellowship with Christ in suffering was his life-long commitment. This was his perspective of suffering "for the sake of His body, that is, the church." Nobody has ever suffered to the extent Jesus suffered. *Paul would not suffer equal to the Savior, but he would suffer like and with the Savior.*

Paul's next statement assures his readers of how he viewed his work and the suffering that accompanied that work. He became a minister "according to the stewardship from God, that was given to" him for this purpose: "...to make the Word of God fully known."

God gave Paul this task and held him accountable, "to make the Word of God fully known." When beginning reading from the epistles, I often say: THIS IS FROM GOD THROUGH PAUL TO...and I name the recipients.

"The mystery hidden for ages and generations" was now being made known to men like Paul, for faithful transmission to others. "To them, God chose to make known how great among the Gentiles are the riches of the glory of this mystery, which is Christ in you, the hope of glory."

The gospel is not a message that Christ is just a part of. Christ is at the center of the message with a generous offer of blessing to all men. As the message is accepted by the activity of faith, Christ is formed in His people with this outcome: "the hope of glory."

So Paul rejoiced (though he suffered) to announce, "Him we proclaim, warning everyone and teaching everyone with all wisdom, that we may present everyone mature in Christ."

The repetitious "everyone" leaves no doubt of the universal scope of the gospel of Christ. God designed and delivered this message of salvation for "everyone" to hear, believe, and obey. This was so important to Paul that he said: "For this I toil, struggling with all His energy that He powerfully works within me."

ANOTHER LOOK!

A TEMPLE NOT MADE WITH HANDS

Alienation, hostility, evil deeds—the unenviable list of rebellion against our Creator is long. The blemishes of sin mar the beauty of the risen Lord. Minds set on things below operate on their own. The bleak picture of sin should make us feel uncomfortable. Even though we have used our lives (bodies) in slavery to sin, Christ used His body to save us. "Yet He has now reconciled you in His fleshly body through death, in order to present you before Him holy and blameless and beyond reproach" (Colossians 1:22 NASB 95). A body was prepared for God's Son (Hebrews 10:5). The body that hung on the cross was not just a fleshly body nailed to pieces of wood; the blood that poured forth on that eventful day was the perfect blood, the perfect sacrifice. Life is in the blood (Leviticus 17:11); Jesus gave His life for you and me.

Public religion was important in Roman society. Protection from enemies came from allegiance to Jupiter, Juno, and Minerva. Temples dedicated to these protecting gods were constructed at a great price to Rome's populace. Never mind that only the elites of Rome could afford to attend the dedications and liturgies that honored these gods. The entire city benefitted when pigs, sheep, and oxen were sacrificed; when famine, war, and plagues came, Rome's citizens were shielded from disaster. If the mortals failed to give to the immortals, the anger of the gods ensued. While there was great fluidity among pagan religions, and while most (presumably) relished the comforting care of their gods, these false gods produced fear. How could true comfort be found in a capricious god? (*The Patient Ferment of the Early Church: The Improbable Rise of Christianity in the Roman Empire*, Kreider, 37-44). Colossae was an important city in the Roman Empire. Located on a major trade route, the city flourished from commerce, both east and west. Was there paganism in Colossae? "Numismatic evidence points most frequently to the worship of the Ephesian Artemis and the Laodicean Zeus..." (*The Anchor Bible Dictionary*, Vol. 1, A-C, 1089).

Any doctrine that degrades Christ is dangerous. The Colossians, living in the shadow of pagan temples, were challenged to acknowledge Christ as Supreme. Christ, who is greater than the temple, invites all to gather with Him. Paul told the Ephesians they were "the whole building, being fitted together...a holy temple in the Lord." We do not need Rome to build a temple for us. We already have one!

Randy Harshbarger

DAY 6

Read: Colossians 2:1-5

This passage is one of those places where Paul opens his heart, wanting Christians to know how he felt. Please observe this "struggle" or passionate concern for Christians was not limited to those he knew personally but also those who had not seen him face to face.

What was this about? Paul wanted their hearts to be encouraged. He wanted them to be knit together in love—"to reach all the riches of full assurance of understanding and the knowledge of God's mystery, which is Christ."

He wanted growth in knowledge and assurance—in their appreciation of who Christ is and what He did. Paul wanted Christians to hold close all those connected truths about Christ in chapter one.

And, of Christ, Paul says that in Him, "are hidden all the treasures of wisdom and knowledge."

The word "hidden" doesn't mean you can't find it. It means *located and protected in Christ and only in Him*. In false teaching, you find deception, destruction, apostasy, spiritual poverty, and loss. In Christ, "are hidden" all the opposites, summarized in this phrase, "all the treasures of wisdom and knowledge."

The false teachers boasted of having some secret way to reach some higher spiritual level. They claimed to have the wisdom Christians needed to be better than others. But it was a lie.

One of the primary themes in Colossians is—all you need can be found in Christ! As it says later in this context, "in Him the whole fullness of deity dwells bodily," and "you have been filled in Him."

There is complete provision for all spiritual needs in Christ. No human supplement or secret is necessary, and all such "philosophy" is an intrusion that leads to loss!

Why is Paul so passionate about this? "I say this in order that no one may delude you with plausible arguments." He doesn't want anyone to be deceived by persuasive words. See, words may sound good but be wrong!

Paul wanted to form a close relationship with the Christians in Colossae and Laodicea—not to firm up his fan base; not for social enjoyment. He wanted them to know this: "For though I am absent in body, yet I am with you in spirit, rejoicing to see your good order and the firmness of your faith in Christ."

ANOTHER LOOK!

LET NO ONE DELUDE YOU

Paul was an unusual person. Before meeting his Savior on the Damascus Road, he inflicted much misery on those of the Way. Now, he rejoiced in his sufferings; he was happy to endure personal trials and tribulations for the benefit of the Colossians. He labored "mightily" to "present every man perfect in Christ Jesus" (Colossians 1:24-29 NASB 95). Paul's "great conflict" was not an exercise in self-pity; he aimed to encourage and instruct the Colossians in "the knowledge of the mystery of God, both of the Father and of Christ" (Colossians 2:1-3).

Citizens in the Roman world knew about athletic contests. Athletes strained, groaned, and agonized in pursuit of victory. Paul sought a victory, too. His prize was to help his brethren understand the spiritual completeness found only in Christ. The unfolding of God's mystery in His Son was a long time in coming. Now, enemies were deluding Christ's completeness. Paul warned against these deceivers, "I say this so that no one will delude you with persuasive argument" (Colossians 2:4).

One thing that would help the Colossians was "hearts knitted together in love." Greg Beale said: "Heart in the NT, and here, likely has the same notion as in the OT: it represents the inner spiritual center of one's relationship with God, which is inextricably linked to the volitional, intellectual, and emotional aspects of a person" (*Colossians and Philemon, Baker Exegetical Commentary on the New Testament*, Beale, 154). Completeness in Christ means that our hearts grow in knowledge; our love must grow, too.

The prophets of old anxiously wanted to know when the Messiah would come (1 Peter 1:10-12). The mystery, rather than being something incomprehensible and esoteric, was something yet to be fully, completely revealed. The word secret, if used, must be explained. God's plans and purposes were not completely unknown but were gradually revealed, with hints along the way, hints that culminated in the ultimate expression of God's will, Christ. The New Testament's use of mystery is often connected to the eschatological kingdom. Could an Old Testament passage such as Daniel 2:19-21 point us in that same direction? "Then the mystery was revealed to Daniel in a night vision. Then Daniel blessed the God of heaven; Daniel said, 'Let the name of God be blessed forever and ever, for wisdom and power belong to Him. It is He who changes the times and the epochs; He removes kings and establishes kings; He gives wisdom to wise men and knowledge to men of understanding.'" Nebuchadnezzar's kingdom would fall, giving way to future kingdoms that soon fell.

Paul said: I am willing to suffer for God's kingdom, for His mystery, for His people, and for the Savior of the world. Are we?

Randy Harshbarger

DAY 7

Read: Colossians 2:6-7

This seemingly neutral word, "therefore," can become an important key to good Bible reading and study. I heard someone once say, "When you see the word 'therefore' in the Bible, stop and observe what it is there for!" That's more than just a play on words.

The term is a connection word—connecting what it introduces with the previous context. A series of arguments or affirmations are made, and then a conclusion is stated.

So, what does this mean in personal, practical terms? THEREFORE—just as you received Christ Jesus the Lord, so WALK IN HIM. Based on all the teaching prior to "therefore," what should the reader do? WALK IN HIM. Live as He illustrated and taught, personally and through the apostles.

The Bible here speaks of receiving Christ Jesus the Lord. It is appropriate for us today to speak of receiving Christ Jesus the Lord. In fact, we should be inclined to teach people from the Bible, and doing what the Bible says constitutes receiving Christ Jesus the Lord. It should never become just a phrase we use with no specific definition. It means exactly what the Bible says it means.

The book of Acts enlightens us. When a sinner understands his/her guilt (Example: Acts 2:23), believes in Christ (Acts 2:36, 8:37), repents and submits to baptism (Acts 2:38), that person has received Jesus Christ the Lord – not just to be forgiven and taken out of sin to God; but to live with Him as the Lord of daily life. One's baptism begins life in the Kingdom of Christ, living under His authority.

Receiving Jesus Christ as Lord means you leave sin and start obeying Him. Then, going forward, ⇨ Walk in Him. "Therefore, as you received Christ Jesus the Lord, so walk in Him." Read again what Paul wrote in the first five verses of the chapter. If those things are true, those who have received Jesus Christ as their Lord should get up every day and walk in Him.

This walk—this way of thinking and living—will bring divine strength into your life. As you walk in Him, you will discover that you are "rooted and built up in Him and established in the faith, just as you were taught, abounding in thanksgiving."

ANOTHER LOOK!

SHACKLED TO CHRIST

"Therefore, as you have received Christ Jesus the Lord, so walk in Him, having been firmly rooted and now being built up in Him and established in your faith, just as you were instructed, and overflowing with gratitude" (Colossians 2:6-7). How could Paul walk with the Lord when he was shackled to a Roman soldier?

Assumptions about the supposed value of Gnosticism (sometimes referred to as the *Colossian-Heresy*) drove many away from the spiritual completeness that only Christ could provide. Reincarnations of the Old Law, worshiping angels, and abusing the body were vain attempts to fill a void that only Christ could fill. Ancient, insignificant ruins of a once important city should remind seekers today that only in Christ are we complete. Calvinistic concerns aside, remember Augustine's *Confessions*: "You have made us for yourself, O Lord, and our hearts are restless until they rest in you."

When we receive Christ, we acknowledge Him to be who He said He is; as Colossians 1:18 says, Christ is the head of the body, the church. We are walking with Him, side by side. He is Lord of all; He has all power; He is in control. Spiritual Peripatetics walk with the Lord, following His lead. We are rooted in Christ; our spiritual foundation goes deep into Him—His love, His desire for our salvation, and His power. Uproot the root, and what remains? Only a mere shadow (Colossians 2:17). We build our lives on Christ; He is our foundation (Matthew 16:16-18). In Christ, our faith is firmly established. We have the sure foundation of Christ on which to base our lives. Paul, Epaphras, and others taught the Colossians God's will. The Word of God dwells in those who have received Christ; the only way to receive Him is to obey His will. We are thankful for the overflowing, bountiful love of Christ.

Most of us do not understand much at all about Paul's imprisonment. We have glimpses in the New Testament. Being beaten and then being thrown into jail, languishing in a dark, dank prison, shivering from the cold and the loneliness of friends—Paul suffered. Still, he prayed for open doors, for opportunities to speak about Jesus. His roots in Jesus ran deep. Do ours? The winds of prisons, enemies, deprivations, and persecutions blew strong against the aged Apostle Paul. But he was not blown away. Why? Because he was shackled to Jesus. Are you?

Randy Harshbarger

DAY 8

Read: Colossians 2:8-10

When an apostle of Christ says, "See to it" or "beware," we should make certain we understand the thrust of the warning. This isn't like some figurative phrase tucked away in Ezekiel or Revelation (that is part of a larger picture and doesn't lend itself to a specific interpretation). This is an apostle of Christ warning Christians then and today: Beware. See to this.

Don't let anyone *take you captive*. There isn't any question; our general disposition is, "I'm not letting anyone take me somewhere against my will. I will not be a victim of kidnapping or enslavement. Nobody will hold me hostage." Good for you. But this is not about physically moving you against your will. In fact, this isn't about any movement against your will. This is about letting your guard down about your faith and letting someone lead you off-center, away from what is confirmed apostolic teaching. The NIV says, "See to it that no one takes you captive through hollow and deceptive philosophy, which depends on human tradition and the elemental spiritual forces of this world rather than on Christ."

As one who has obeyed Christ in repentance and baptism, therefore devoted to walking in Him (verse 6), I must guard against anyone leading me away from Him into some hollow, deceptive system of thought that came from man, not God. This is what Jesus warned about in Matthew 7. "Beware of false prophets," or "look out for false prophets."

As a Christian, you are a servant of God and a follower of Christ, joined with others in your spiritual family to glorify God, preach to the lost, and serve your family. You are in submission to divine authority in all relationships and aspects of life.

You are not in submission to anyone who comes along with some new twist of doctrine, popular philosophy, or eye-catching trending innovation. Beware. There are charming false teachers. There are spiritual radicals who want to "explode" local churches. Religious terrorists, who do not use literal guns but cleverly disguised error, are loaded with false teaching, temptation, and selfish agendas. Beware.

Philosophy simply means a system of thought. The modern corresponding term could be "world view." There were systems of thought (like Gnostism) in the first century that attempted to combine pagan assertions with the gospel.

Empty deceit points to that which is futile, vain, and not according to Christ.

Human tradition is about what men come up with and pass on, which is contrary to the truth of Christ. Human tradition is often sold to the naïve based on the life of the tradition: "This has been so for a long time. You just have missed it."

The elemental spirits of the world may have reference to ancient, crude rules and regulations men came up with, which are based in the world, rather than what comes from the Creator of the world. The background may be that ugly realm Paul refers to as "the spiritual forces of evil in the heavenly places" (Eph. 6:12).

Here's a simple rule we can apply. If something we hear, see, or read is "not according to Christ," don't have any part of it. "Take no part in the unfruitful works of darkness, but instead expose them" (Eph. 5:11).

Christ and His teaching protect us. And His teaching in the New Testament is perfectly sufficient! "For in Him the whole fullness of deity dwells bodily, and you have been filled in Him, who is the head of all rule and authority."

These two verses (Col. 2:9,10) punctuate one of the primary themes of Colossians. In Christ, we have all we need to get out of sin, have fellowship with God, live a righteous life, and go to heaven. So, if something is "not according to Christ," reject it! It deserves to be rejected, no matter who the deliverer is. For instance, a man may be charming, likeable, friendly, and have a professional countenance—but be corrupt in what he is teaching.

To know if something is "not according to Christ," you'll have to learn who Christ is and what He said, as revealed by the apostles. That means, get your head into the New Testament and read it over and over. Go to Bible classes where God's Word is taught. Never let repetition bore you (Phil. 3:1). Knowing the truth of Christ is your defense against those who could take you captive.

ANOTHER LOOK!

FULLNESS IN CHRIST

"For it was the Father's good pleasure for all the fullness to dwell in Him" (Colossians 1:19 NASB 95). "For in Him all the fullness of Deity dwells in bodily form" (Colossians 2:9).

"Furthermore, it is 'in Him' (Christ), as Colossians puts it, that 'all the fullness of God dwells bodily (Col. 2:9 MJG; cf. 1:19), and thus it is 'in Him' that 'you are completely fulfilled' (Col. 2:10 MJG). As in 2 Corinthians 5:14-21, according to Colossians, the incarnation was for the purpose of reconciliation through the cross (Col. 1:20). In other words, the incarnation of God and the cross of Christ are inseparable; to be Godlike and thus 'full' as a human being, then, will mean to be cross-like" (*Participating in Christ: Explorations in Paul's Theology and Spirituality*, Gorman, Michael J. 10-11).

The Apostle Paul would never deny the centrality of Jesus' cross for the salvation of humanity. The cross was dominant in Paul's preaching (1 Corinthians 2:2). His life was the outgrowth of God's grace (1 Corinthians 15:10). The Colossians would feel the same way, wouldn't they? Yet, they were in danger of being duped and cheated by offers of a higher, more spiritual existence. Paul challenged the false teachers by pointing the Colossians to Christ, His cross, and the cross-like life they could live. What does that life look like?

Would recognizing Christ as our spiritual head, as head of His church, His body, help us understand how we should and can live? It was the Father's will that His Son represent heaven's will on earth; hence, the incarnation and the cross. The result: His church (of course, there are other Bible teachings that speak about our relationship with Jesus; think kingdom, temple, family). A relationship, yes, but a functional relationship. As members of the body, we recognize the authority of our Head. As members of the body, we relish the connection to our Head. We may be a more easily noticed member of the body or we may be weaker members of the body; we are ALL still members of His body! And we all have something to contribute. That togetherness would help the Colossians rally around the cross in service to their Master and serving the world they lived in. The cross identifies those who come to the Savior in humility, in hope, and in search of forgiveness. His resurrection gives us assurance.

The Gnostics said: Climb the rungs of our spiritual ladder. You will be more spiritual and more attuned to the world. Or we can walk the hill to Mount Calvary. What do we see? A crucified, torn, suffering Savior, a body falling apart? Look again. There is completeness in Jesus!

Randy Harshbarger

DAY 9

Read: Colossians 2:11-15

In Ephesians and Colossians, this repeated phrase carries great meaning: "In Him." This is about one's relationship with God through or in Jesus Christ. The penitent believer is baptized "into" Christ (see Gal. 3:27 and Rom. 6:1-4). Once in that relationship, the present and eternal benefits of God's grace are enjoyed, unless one abandons Christ (2 Pet. 2:21,22).

Under consideration in Colossians 2:11 is repentance—depicted in Jewish terms—as "putting off the body of the flesh" or "the circumcision of Christ." Paul is reminding the saints in Colossae of a past act that should continue to have a present influence on their behavior.

To the Jews, circumcision was an act of removal that brought the individual into the covenant. Likewise, figuratively speaking, when one repents and is baptized into Christ—in that activity of faith, ideally—sin is removed. It is forgiven, and the forgiven person gives it up. Paul uses this Jewish imagery to emphasize the new life in Christ.

He wants Christians in Colossae to remember they were "buried with Christ in baptism" and raised with Him through faith to a new life. This powerful working of God—they accepted when they obeyed the gospel. Before their baptism, they were "dead" in "trespasses" and "the uncircumcision of their flesh." Now, because of God's grace and Christ's death, they embraced repentance and baptism—the old debt was canceled. "Having forgiven us all our trespasses."

The guilt of sin and the Old Law of Moses that drove that guilt into their hearts was NAILED TO THE CROSS! Charges of guilt under the old law were fastened to the cross. The guilt of sin is erased not by keeping a law nailed to the cross. The guilt of sin is erased when the penitent believer is "buried with" Christ "in baptism."

Also, at the cross, the demonic forces of evil so dramatic in the life of Christ were—*disarmed by the death of Christ*, and "put to open shame."

This paragraph is about victory. The old fleshly rite of circumcision no longer held spiritual authority. What mattered now for all men was repentance and baptism, with the new life that God intended.

That is exactly what matters for Christians today. When you repented and were buried with Christ in baptism, you entered into a new life. The Old Law of Moses was nailed to the cross; the demons were disarmed and we are free to live under the New Covenant of Jesus Christ. Every day!

ANOTHER LOOK!

A CIRCUMCISION WITHOUT HANDS

"And in Him you were also circumcised with a circumcision made without hands, in the removal of the body of the flesh by the circumcision of Christ; having been buried with Him in baptism, in which you were also raised up with Him through faith in the working of God, who raised Him from the dead. When you were dead in your transgressions and the uncircumcision of your flesh, He made you alive together with Him, having forgiven us all our transgressions" (Colossians 2:11-13 NASNB 95).

Consider Lightfoot's comments: "The distinguishing features of this higher circumcision are threefold. (1) It is not external but inward, not made with hands but wrought by the Spirit. (2) It divests not a part only of the flesh, but the whole body of carnal affections. (3) It is the circumcision— not of Moses or the patriarchs, but of Christ. Thus, it is distinguished, as regards first its *character*, secondly its *extent*, and thirdly its *author*" (*St. Paul's Epistles to the Colossians and Philemon*, Lightfoot, J.B., Hendrickson, 183).

The character of something is what something is. A theatrical performance might be described as romantic, humorous, or morbid. Paul describes a circumcision that seeks and has as its goal inward transformation. The old man of sin is buried and left behind; this is like the "put on" and "take off" language in Colossians three. The extent of this circumcision is that the whole man is involved, not just a part of one's physical body. Obeying from the heart means the entirety of oneself is given in obedience to Christ in the act of baptism. The command is given by Christ, the author of baptism. No one else can give validity to the efficaciousness of baptism.

Christ was circumcised according to "the custom of the law" in the temple, on the eighth day of His young existence (see Luke chapter two). Mary and Joseph obeyed according to the law. Simeon held the baby in his arms and saw salvation for the entire world. Anna spoke of redemption for Israel. Mary, Joseph, and Jesus went home. "The Child continued to grow and become strong, increasing in wisdom; and the grace of God was upon Him" (Luke 2:40).

The circumcision of Christ belongs to Christ. The fullness of life cannot begin or exist apart from Him. In sin, we die; in Christ, we live. But life begins only when the old self of sin is cut off. Will we join the Colossians in obeying the Savior? Randy Harshbarger

42

DAY 10

Read: Colossians 2:16-19

Sometimes the personal criticism we receive from others is constructive. Even if not given with a perfect attitude, what our critic says can help us discover some flaw or sin. When we deal with that (personal correction), we can say that the criticism had value. We should always be open to constructive criticism or judgment.

In some cases, however, our critics are wrong and their ill-conceived judgments should not be taken seriously or applied.

In Colossae, there was a false religious system that was being advanced that included *judging people negatively without any basis given by God*.

For example, if someone says to me: "You are telling lies," and I am guilty—that judgment is based on God's requirement of honesty. I should take that seriously because of the origin of the principle I'm violating.

However, if someone says to me: "You are not observing the religious days my religious calendar dictates?" Or, "You are not eating what I religiously consume. Your menu is not like mine?" We should not take seriously or apply those judgments: "*let no one pass judgment on you*" in these matters—where God has not spoken. God is the One who gets to set the standard not us.

There were various precepts and observances of a former generation still being imposed on Christians in Colossae. It created confusion for new Christians and agitation for others. A false view of what being a Christian is all about was being vigorously promoted. In this passage, it is like Paul saying: Don't let them tell you what to do. They (the false teachers in Colossae) do not set the standard. God has revealed what you should do through Christ and His apostles. It is not just a matter of people being mis-guided or false teachers being aggressive. If we let these human impositions govern us, we sever our relationship with our Head, Jesus Christ.

You can't serve Christ alongside other masters. You can't follow His teaching and attempt to supplement His teaching with the vain imaginations that come from the minds of men who have self-serving agendas.

As members of the body of Christ, we receive our nourishment from Him. Doctrines and commandments of men do not nourish us, but can, when believed and obeyed, take us away from our true Head.

So, let no one judge you or disqualify you. Hold fast to the Head!

ANOTHER LOOK!

TRUE VALUE

In Colossians chapter two particularly, Paul continues his stinging critique of the pseudo teachers with their vain philosophies and persuasive arguments. Attempts to undermine the completeness Jesus provides were real; they were real in the sense that if the Colossians were not careful, they could be tempted to let go of Christ "the head." Letting go leaves one adrift on the sandbars of error and destruction. Are you sure about that Paul? Yes, I am sure. Do not be deceived by what seems to be true; it is only a shadow; you need the substance.

The Dead Sea Scrolls tell us about the Essenes (the Pious Ones), an austere Jewish community dedicated to fasting and celebrations pertaining to the Law of Moses. They were extreme in their practices and quickly excluded any who resisted such stringent activities. They lived in Qumran near Jericho and Engedi. The Sabbath was of special importance. They rejected the resurrection of the body; any afterlife was completely spiritual in nature. Some communities embraced marriage; others rejected marriage unless the one and only purpose was procreation (*The Complete Dead Sea Scrolls in English*, Geza Vermes, The Penguin Press, 46-47).

We could assume that Paul is striking against the ascetic life of these marginal, splinter groups. Colossians 2:16 says: "Therefore no one is to act as your judge in regard to food or drink or in respect to a festival or a new moon or a Sabbath day." Yet, there is little emphasis from Paul on the Law, at least with specificity. Is the background of Colossians painted with Jewish or Hellenistic colors, or both? Paul's "Therefore" points the Colossians away from the Law because the Law was taken away. Paul's "Therefore" takes the Colossians away from special diets and special days. Paul's "Therefore" takes the Colossians away from the shadow and points them to reality.

Where does Paul's "Therefore" take you and me? The only answer is to Christ, the reality. We live by faith, not by "matters which have, to be sure, the appearance of wisdom in self-made religion and self-abasement and severe treatment of the body but are of no value against fleshly indulgence" (Colossians 2:23 NASB 95). Laws of human origin have no higher standard than "will worship." Things may look good; you may even feel good about your attempts at greater spirituality. Do not be deceived. Christ alone is *the true value*. Randy Harshbarger

DAY 11

Read: Colossians 2:20-23

"If with Christ you have died" is a reference to their conversion to Christ. These Christians in Colossae are reminded of their choice to leave sin (die to it) and become followers of Christ. Romans 6 teaches one dies with Christ in baptism (See also Col. 2:12). So here (Col. 2:20), Paul takes their attention back to that initial act of dying with Christ—the implications of that act needed to be considered as they were tempted and deceived by false teachers.

In that initial act of obedience, they died with Christ "to the elemental spirits of the world." In conversion, they separated themselves from the worldly, the earthly ideas and ambitions, the human wisdom now being pushed in their face by false teachers.

The main question of this text is—if you have given up those earthly elemental forms and patterns, why now—as baptized believers—would you go back and let men subject you to human religious regulations?

"If you died with Christ, as, of course, you did," for you were buried with Him (see verse 12 above) and you were raised with Him (verse 12 again; also 3:1), then you have also in that very act made a complete break with all such rudimentary instruction that bases its hope upon anything apart from Christ and fullness of salvation in Him.[1]

The false teachers at work in Colossae had developed (or received from their religious forefathers) a set of rules they were imposing and pushing. Paul is telling the Christians in Colossae you are complete in Christ! You died to those things.

"Do not handle?" "Do not taste?" "Do not touch?" These human precepts were worldly, perishable, and human in origin. They referred to things "that all perish as they are used." If you have died with Christ in baptism (2:12), you have walked away from such human religious regulations.

---

[1] Hendriksen, W., & Kistemaker, S. J. (1953- 2001). Vol. 6: Exposition of Colossians and Philemon. New Testament Commentary (130). Grand Rapids: Baker Book House.

"These have indeed an appearance of wisdom in promoting self-made religion and asceticism and severity to the body, but they are of no value in stopping the indulgence of the flesh."

The religious rules and regulations men invented and pushed—might look impressive. But the system was self-made, made by the user rather than the Creator.

Asceticism is a system of thought (man-made) that treats the body severely, assuming this has some deep spiritual benefit. False teachers in Colossae were pushing this, but Paul is clear: "They are of no value in stopping the indulgence of the flesh."

So, how do we get out of sin and into fellowship with God? How do we develop long-term self-control? Where do we find wisdom for good living and with solid hope as we face death?

In Christ "are hidden all the treasures of wisdom and knowledge," (Col. 2:3).

ANOTHER LOOK!

SELF-MADE RELIGION

"Do not handle, do not taste, do not touch!" (which all refer to things destined to perish with use)—are in accordance with the commandments and teachings of men. These are matters which have, to be sure, the appearance of wisdom in self-made religion and self-abasement and severe treatment of the body but are of no value against fleshly indulgence" (Colossians 2:21-23 NASB 95).

False teachers wanted to supplement Paul's teaching. They insisted that denying the needs of the body or the severe abuse and misuse of the body were spiritual activities that would elevate the practitioner to a higher level of wisdom and completeness. Some things were not to be handled; this would help to curb any practice that diluted rather than encouraged one's quest for a higher echelon of spirituality. Rise higher and worship the angels; they would bring you closer to God.

Efforts, however sincere or not, to attain a higher spiritual level could find some support or connection to Old Testament passages. For example, 2 Chronicles 29:5: "Then he said to them, "Listen to me, O Levites. Consecrate yourselves now, and consecrate the house of the Lord, the God of your fathers, and carry the uncleanness out from the holy place." Uncleanness would contaminate the temple, thus perverting true worship; leaving off uncleanness in any form is good. Paul, though, says that the efforts of these false teachers were nothing more than the commandments and teachings of men. This alludes to Isaiah 29:13: "Then the Lord said, because this people draw near with their words and honor Me with their lip service, but they remove their hearts far from Me, and their reverence for Me consists of tradition learned by rote." Isaiah strikes against the failure of Israel to honor God; the result was idolatry; the worship of idols is in vain. "Behold, all of them are false; Their works are worthless, their molten images are wind and emptiness" (Isaiah 41:29).

Our desires and our motivations must focus on Christ. Why turn to angels or dreams when Christ, the true reality, is the image of the invisible God? Why make the mistake of believing that spiritual forces, principalities, and powers are any match for God? Christ is our head; anything else is a mere shadow. Substituting man-made will worship for Christ can only lead to despair and hopelessness. The lure of the modern "self" is strong, but our own selfish desires distort rather than transform. Prideful hearts say: We want to do this! This will make us happy! Surely, the Lord will accept what we do because we want to do so! Remember: Anything or anyone other than Christ is of no value.

Randy Harshbarger

DAY 12

Read: Colossians 3:1-4

In the previous paragraph (2:20), we found the expression, "If with Christ you died," and connected it with their initial response to the gospel in baptism (back to 2:12). To die with Christ is to penitently give up the sin that has killed you and joyfully and obediently embrace the spiritual life that God makes available in Christ.

Here is an expression that has that same connection, "If you have been raised with Christ."

When a lost person hears the gospel and is moved by the death, burial, and resurrection of Christ, their response bears a resemblance to those historical truths (see Rom. 6:1-4). We are buried with Christ in baptism and "raised from the dead" to "walk in newness of life." This is all about one's initial responses to the gospel, then one's intentional participation (walk) with spiritual death in the rear-view mirror.

So here in chapter three of Colossians, "if you have been raised with Christ" is equivalent to if you have become a Christian, if you are a baptized believer.

If you are, there is this everyday life direction: *seeking the things that are above, where Christ is, seated at the right hand of God.*

Your thought patterns are not scattered, random, or worldly. You have in mind—all the time—this joyful seeking of the things that are above. Your heart is fixed in this direction. Therefore, your life moves in this heavenly direction.

In verse 2, this becomes imperative: "Set your minds on things that are above, not on things that are on earth." If your mind is filled with considerations of things limited to this earth, and you have to make a little room to think about God and "go to church" and pray a little (especially when you are stressed), your life isn't fixed where it needs to be. "Set your mind on things that are above, not on things that are on earth."

Why? "For you have died, and your life is hidden with Christ in God." Again, "you have died" is a reference to one's initial response to Christ (see again, Col. 2:12 with Rom. 6:1-4). If you have made that choice, your life after baptism must have this solid heavenly direction. You do want to finish what you started, right? "Therefore, we must pay much closer attention to what we have heard, lest we drift away from it," (Heb. 2:1).

"Your life is hidden with Christ in God." This doesn't mean you are invisible, out of sight, or not connected to people. The word "hidden" here carries the idea of protection. Those who walk with Christ are protected by Him and "hidden" with Him "in God." While this fellowship depends on your initial and continued response to Christ (see Col. 2:6,7), what is assured here is protection, safety, and intimacy with deity.

> *You have been raised to life with Christ. Now set your heart on what is in heaven, where Christ rules at God's right side. Think about what is up there, not about what is here on earth. You died, which means that your life is hidden with Christ, who sits beside God. Christ gives meaning to your life, and when he appears, you will also appear with him in glory. (NIV)*

And this mindset has hope: "When Christ, who is your life, appears, then you also will appear with Him in glory."

This is really a "way of life" passage and—behind that—a "way of thinking" passage. This way of thinking and living will be consummated in a glorious way "when He comes, in that day, to be glorified in His saints and to be admired among all those who believe, because our testimony among you was believed," (2 Thess. 1:10).

ANOTHER LOOK!

SEEK, SET, SEVER, SANCTIFY

"If then you have been raised with Christ, keep looking for the good things of heaven. This is where Christ is seated on the right side of God. Keep your minds thinking about things in heaven. Do not think about things on the earth. You are dead to the things of this world. Your new life is now hidden in God through Christ. Christ is our life. When He comes again, you will also be with Him to share His shining greatness. (Colossians 3:1-4 New Life Version).

Paul now begins driving home needed applications. Christ is supreme and complete; challengers will fail; principalities and powers have been disarmed. What do we do? Paul says: *Seek, Set, Sever, and Sanctify*. We were raised with Christ in baptism; now, washed clean by His blood, we can live a completely new life, a life not possible before. With circumcised hearts, we have a new direction for the high call of the gospel. Can we agree that Paul was serious about his life before and after he met Christ on the Damascus Road? As never before, his focus became Christ; this is the one thing he did (read Philippians 3).

We are no longer in bondage to the weak and beggarly elements of this world; our newfound liberty in Christ lifts our heads in faith and fortitude. And why not? The old man is in the grave; we are citizens of the kingdom of heaven. Living by faith, we see what is to come. False teachers claimed to "see," but they were "intruding" into the unknown. Christ is our life, both now and for eternity. What we have in Christ is not a secret; it is profound, yes, but we can know Christ and Him crucified. He is at His Father's right hand (is Paul thinking about Psalm 110:1? "The Lord says to my Lord: 'Sit at My right hand until I make Your enemies a footstool for Your feet'"). One greater than David is on the throne. One greater than any Gnostic demi-urge is on the throne. Let us put Christ on the throne in our hearts.

Note: I am indebted to my friend and par excellent preacher Curtis Pope for the four words that begin this small piece. I do not remember where I was or when I heard his lesson on this passage; I just know I did and that I got it from him and gladly give him credit.

Randy Harshbarger

DAY 13

Read: Colossians 3:5-8

Carefully follow the train of thought here. If you have been "buried with Christ in baptism" (2:12) and "raised with Christ," – you are (1) seeking the things above [v.2], and you are (2) executing what is earthly in you [v.5].

"Put to death therefore what is earthly in you," (verse 5). What is earthly in you is not some physical dirt that can be physically cleansed. What is earthly is what is specified in this context as all that is impure in the sight of God. We live on earth, but we must not be "earthly."

As one "buried with Christ in baptism" and "raised with Christ," you are not only authorized to perform these necessary "executions" but mandated. Whatever is worldly, sinful, unsuitable for heaven – you should – as soon as you see it in you – Kill It.

Don't schedule an execution date in the future (delayed justice). As soon as you discover what is earthly in your mind and life – Pull the Trigger. For examples:

Sexual immorality is any and all sexual activity with anyone outside a legitimate marriage. When you find yourself in that sin, stop and repent. "Put to death" sexual immorality.

Impurity is any thought, thought patterns, words, or actions that contradict the purity God expects of His people. When it comes to your attention, pull the trigger.

Passion is burning and boiling excitement for something not worthy of your energy. Kill it.

Evil desire has to do with one's interest in what is wrong. Put it to death.

Covetousness, which is idolatry, is wanting something with such unreasonable drive you are willing to reject God and "make an idol" to have what you want. Put that to death too.

Why? "On account of these, the wrath of God is coming." If God objects to these things and has promised to react negatively (the wrath of God is coming), I need to identify and execute these sins. Because of Jesus' death and resurrection, I can trust and obey Him and then carry out these necessary executions. God's grace enables us to carry out these drastic actions and motivates us to do so.

Verse 7: "In these you too once walked, when you were living in them." Before obeying the gospel, you may have embraced and lived in all these sins.

"But now you must put them all away..." Before conversion, we not only accepted these things, we fed them. Now we must uproot them, kill them, and put them away (which sounds much like the language of divorce).

Commercials use obscenity to market their products. The majority of entertainment uses sexual innuendo and suggestion, bathroom humor, and irreverent speaking of God – as a part of their praised products offered to the public. National leaders feel pressured to include obscenity in their language. The school hallways and business offices buzz with filthy language.

The person who has been buried with Christ in baptism rejects these popular ways of communication, to preserve what is pure and righteous.

"Put them all away." To be a Christian requires necessary executions.

You once lived in these things, "but now..." Now that you have been buried with Christ in baptism and raised with Him to see the things above – PUT THEM ALL AWAY.

Anger is an unreasonable emotional reaction that goes beyond natural disappointment with someone or something. Wrath is an additional step into a destructive emotional reaction. Malice is devotion to injury, a desire to hurt or get someone back. Slander is ill-conceived and unjustified words against someone (generally connected to anger, wrath, and malice).

"And obscene talk from your mouth" must be rejected by those who have been buried with Christ in baptism.

ANOTHER LOOK!

MORTIFICATION

"Therefore, consider the members of your earthly body as dead to immorality, impurity, passion, evil desire, and greed, which amounts to idolatry. For it is because of these things that the wrath of God will come upon the sons of disobedience, and in them you also once walked, when you were living in them. But now you also, put them all aside: anger, wrath, malice, slander, and abusive speech from your mouth" (Colossians 3:5-8 NASB 95).

It is likely that the Christians in Colossae were young in the faith; this could easily be true of many Christians in the locations mentioned by Paul—places he traveled to, preaching and converting people, and then leaving behind a called-out people. The world these new Christians left behind was (is) remarkedly like our world today; they do, and we do, still live in this world. Yes, they were free from sin. United with Christ, being buried with Him in baptism, and then raised to walk with Him, the challenges of their world would remain. In fact, their pursuit of things above only intensified. They could leave the old man behind; quick fixes, though, could leave these saints struggling once again with their past lives. Paul said: Don't forget the false teachers. "See to it that no one takes you captive through philosophy and empty deception, according to the tradition of men, according to the elementary principles of the world, rather than according to Christ" (Colossians 2:8). Don't be duped into believing that pseudo-spiritual practices protect you from the devil. "These are matters which have, to be sure, the appearance of wisdom in self-made religion and self-abasement and severe treatment of the body but are of no value against fleshly indulgence" (Colossians 2:23). Their newfound identity came from Christ; He is in heaven; seek Him first.

In our beginning passage, we can count at least ten actions and/or attitudes that must be mortified. Every sin must be considered and dealt with; none can be ignored. Our public and our private lives are to be controlled by the Spirit of God. Spiritual determination becomes a strong weapon in our spiritual arsenal. Call sin what it is—SIN! Covetousness is idolatry; bowing before a heart of greed is just as bad as bowing before the idols that lined the streets of Colossae. Sin brings God's wrath; in other words, sin is BAD! Don't think of unbelievers right now; think about yourself. The old man is inconsistent with the new man in Christ. Put sin to death; refuse it, starve it, reject it. Can mortification be painful? Yes!

But there is no other way. Do you need to conduct a funeral today?

Randy Harshbarger

DAY 14

Read: Colossians 3:9-15

Preachers have forever said to Christians, "Do not lie." A strong motive is attached to that prohibition: "...seeing that you have put off the old self with its practices and have put on the new self, which is being renewed in knowledge after the image of its Creator."

In other words, since you have been converted from the old to the new. This is a theme in this section of Colossians. You have made a choice God enabled you to make. You have accepted the gift of salvation from Him, made possible by Christ's death. What now? You have changed! Don't go back.

DO NOT LIE. Prohibitions are easier to keep if the stakes are high and the motives are clear. The stakes could not be higher (verse 6), and the motive could not be deeper – I am a Christian; I do not lie! I gave that up.

Here is an important part of this: "...being renewed in knowledge after the image of its Creator." Every day, a Christian continues to be committed to the Lord and is nourished by the Word – knowledge is refined, renewed, and reviewed. It is not like worldly knowledge or philosophy (see 2:8). It is – in origin – "after the image of its Creator." Every word from God reflects and conforms to His divine image. Since we were made in His image (Gen. 1:27), the knowledge we need is the knowledge He imparts in His written revelation. One part of that received knowledge is to avoid dishonesty—"do not lie."

"Here, there is not Greek and Jew, circumcised and uncircumcised, barbarian, Scythian, slave, free; but Christ is all, and in all."

Do you know what an exclusive club is? In the town where I grew up and now reside, there was – and still is – the Hardscrabble Country Club, established in 1926.

When I was a boy, the "social class" we belonged to meant we had no access to Hardscrabble property or venues. You had to have a certain income and status and be nominated and voted on. Until the late 1960s, it was "white only." Some of that has changed in modern times, but membership still costs thousands of dollars, plus a monthly fee. It is—like many others around the country—an exclusive country club.

The Lord's church is not like that! The ill-conceived distinctions so strongly enforced in worldly society have no meaning in Christ. The things that separate people in society – like money, education, race, age, nationality, politics – have no meaning in Christ.

So, there is a beauty of diversity in the body of Christ. One comes into this relationship by being buried with Christ in baptism and raised with Christ (see previous verses 2:12 & 3:1). What you were before doesn't even get in the door!

Buried with Christ in baptism, we are united with Him, no matter how bad we were or how different we are in neutral matters. That's the point of verse eleven.

What does this mean to Christians today? "Put on, then, as God's chosen ones, holy and beloved, compassionate hearts, kindness, humility, meekness, and patience, bearing with one another and, if one has a complaint against another, forgiving each other, as the Lord has forgiven you, so you also must forgive."

Conversion is so well articulated here in the behavior that results. When one is buried with Christ in baptism to be raised with Him into a relationship with God – the ensuing behavior ought to be embraced with joy and become fully apparent. In particular, the dispositional traits identified in verses 12-15. I should not only want to have these virtues in my life, I should want to grow them, adorn them and let them please God and nurture others, but without an advertising campaign. The forgiveness (after the Lord's model of forgiveness) becomes much easier when the related attitudes are embraced. If I am a child of God – part of the elect of God – these are the identifying marks of that life: tenderness, kindness, humility, meekness, and longsuffering.

Remember who you are! As a Christian, you are (1) raised with Christ, (2) "Your life is hidden with Christ in God," (3) you are a new person, and (4) "God's chosen."

"And above all these things, put on love, which binds everything together in perfect harmony. And let the peace of Christ rule in your hearts, to which indeed you were called in one body. And be thankful."

ANOTHER LOOK!

NEW CLOTHES—OLD CLOTHES

Most everyone enjoys buying or receiving new clothes. Some folks are bargain hunters; they enjoy the thrill of finding the right outfits at reduced prices. Some folks hate to shop, doing so only out of necessity. Some people are thankful for what they have; some people are never satisfied with new clothes, new cars, new houses, new spouses, etc. Remember Paul's words about covetousness (see 1 Thessalonians 4:6 for an implied comment about lust and a brother in Christ).

New clothes make us look clean and kept, at least on the outside. If it were only a matter of wearing bright, sparkling outfits, we would be OK. What about the inside? We live in the flesh; we have a biological fleshly existence; yet we must remember that the works of the flesh, the actions, attitudes, and impulses that soil our new clothes, must constantly be "put off." Liberation from sin is what we need, and Christ's sacrifice breaks the bondage of sin; still, the struggles of the flesh do not go away overnight. The desires of the flesh compete against the Spirit. If not careful, we can end up doing the very thing we did not want to do. Sin deceives; it is pretty, flashy, and dangerous; often it has a hook in it. Kill the sin, or it will kill you. "Therefore, consider the members of your earthly body as dead to immorality, impurity, passion, evil desire, and greed, which amounts to idolatry" (Colossians 3:5 NASB 95). New people in Christ have changed clothes. The world we live in is a new world, a heavenly world. We lay aside the old self; we strip off that old clothing. Our former friends do not recognize us. Soon, though, our new identities emerge. Old friends may not approve when they see us wearing Christ in our lives.

"So, as those who have been chosen of God, holy and beloved, put on a heart of compassion, kindness, humility, gentleness and patience" (Colossians 3:12). Because we are seeking heaven, we must make sure our attire reflects that interest. New people in Christ act like new people in Christ. Compassion, kindness, humility, gentleness, and patience are juxtaposed with immorality, impurity, passion, evil desire, and greed. How often did Paul think back to Israel, with all the hopes and promises of a chosen people? "For you are a holy people to the Lord your God; the Lord your God has chosen you to be a people for His own possession out of all the peoples who are on the face of the earth" (Deuteronomy 6:6). We can be holy because our Father and our Savior are holy. That includes the outside and the inside.

Clothes do not make the man or woman! Really? Take it up with the Lord.

Randy Harshbarger

DAY 15

Read: Colossians 3:16-17

The point of becoming a Christian is not simply to identify with a local group. It is not merely to have previous sins forgiven. The point is not to satisfy family and friends who were urging you to become a Christian. While all of this has value – here's the priority: Entering such a close relationship with Christ, His Word lives in you. And, do not just reside there but be activated in your life on the richest level.

Therefore, if the Word of Christ doesn't dwell in you, no matter how large and sound the church is, you are not engaged fully in God's purpose for your life. The Word of Christ must dwell in you richly. No matter how much data you are able to hold in your head (Bible history, dates, memory verses)—no matter how many good people who have surrounded you with encouragement—no matter how many good deeds you have done ⇨ the foundational purpose and ongoing motive is: I live in Christ and His Word lives in me. That makes everything else presently and eternally real.

This point will not have to be argued with those who love Jesus Christ and deeply appreciate the grace of God. Such people will desire that the teaching of Christ dwell in them and govern all their thoughts, words, actions and reactions.

One collective expression of this is singing. "Teaching and admonishing one another in all wisdom, singing psalms and hymns and spiritual songs."

Let me ask—when you first read this verse (Col. 3:16), do you immediately think of a stage band with drums in the background, lead singers and backup singers, pumping music through high-decibel PA speakers to a swaying and dancing audience? Do you really think that's what the apostle Paul had in mind (or the first-century equivalent of popular music to entertain an audience)?

We must guard against letting modern images drive how we read Scripture. It is an interpretative enterprise that is impulsive, and culture-driven, though perhaps popular. What was Paul talking about?

First, he wasn't talking about raw, worldly entertainment, where you listen to music you like and acknowledge the musicians. There is nothing in Colossians 3 or the New Testament to support such an idea.

Second, the very words used by Paul and the context strongly and directly indicate this is worship. It is engaged in by those who are filled with the Word of Christ. It is teaching and admonishing to share wisdom from God, and it is "to God." It is not entertainment to an audience. It is worship to God, shared by people who are filled with the Word of Christ. It is not perfect four-part harmony. It is not perfect pitch and intonation. You do your best to sing your best with the rest, but the spiritual lyrics and your focus on God are the key.

Further, the absence of entertaining instruments leaves us with the simple presence of vocal music: SINGING.

Here is how simple this is: God said sing. Those in whom the Word dwells are satisfied with this because it is what God said. We do this "with thankfulness" in our hearts to God. We reject the off-hand remark, "Sure it says 'sing,' but I think…"

Please, think WORSHIP, not ENTERTAINMENT.

"And, whatever you do, in word or deed, do everything in the name of the Lord Jesus, giving thanks to God the Father through Him."

The simple application of verse 16 – respecting the limits of context—should characterize our understanding and use of all Scripture. So that whatever we do – as individuals, families, local churches—we do as people who belong to the Lord and uphold His name in all we do. May all we do carry the imprint of His authority.

ANOTHER LOOK!

WORSHIP

Colossians 3:16-17: *"Let the word of Christ richly dwell within you, with all wisdom teaching and admonishing one another with psalms and hymns and spiritual songs, singing with thankfulness in your hearts to God. Whatever you do in word or deed, do all in the name of the Lord Jesus, giving thanks through Him to God the Father" (NASV 95).*

In *Early Christians Speak, Faith and Life in the First Three Centuries*, Everett Ferguson gleans evidence from ancient historians who wrote about the early religious practices of some rather odd people—people who would not worship Ceasar, choosing instead to devote their lives to a crucified Messiah. These early "historians" were mostly not favorable to the practices of these early saints; yet their comments add layers of understanding about these early saints, their faith, and their intentions when they gathered for worship. For example, Pliny the Younger, investigating on behalf of Emperor Trajan, said: "[The former Christians] affirmed, however, the whole of their guilt, or their error, was that they were in the habit of meeting on a certain fixed day before it was light, when they sang in alternate verses a hymn to Christ, as to a god, and bound themselves to a solemn oath, not to any wicked deeds..." (Ferguson, 79). Read and evaluate, agree or not, but it is interesting, even encouraging, that we are not the first people to consistently gather each Lord's Day for worship.

Our beginning passage opens vistas of hope and encouragement for the Colossians and 21st-century Christians. Christ gives us peace; yet the necessary correlation is that we let His Word dwell in us. The gospel message reveals Christ to us; the gospel message directs our lives. Truth about Christ is not theoretical; it is practical (cf. James 1:22). When Christ's Word dwells in us, every part and parcel of our lives will be guided by Him. His will is true wisdom. False teachers were anxious to add their own wisdom to Christ's. His wisdom teaches and admonishes us; we, in turn, worship alongside our brothers and sisters and admonish them and ourselves. We sing with thankful hearts. Scriptural worship never loses sight of Christ's Word. His name and authority expressed in His will dictate how we live and worship. Read Colossians 2:23 again.

In recent years, or so it seems to me, interest in improving the singing in congregations has increased. New songs are being written, and new songbooks are available. The content and intent of some, I wonder about. Congregational singings are common. The use of PowerPoint displays of the songs we sing is helpful; at least we are looking up. It seems like it would be hard to sing "Oh, how I love Jesus" with our heads buried in our laps.

The Colossians needed to worship. We do, too. Don't get drunk with wine, sing! Don't lose sight of the Lord; be sober and sing! As my good friend and mentor, Melvin Curry said: "Glorifying God with human voices epitomizes the fellowship all believers should have in Christ" (*True Worship*, Florida College Annual Lectures, 2005, 215). Amen! Let us stand and sing!

Randy Harshbarger

DAY 16
Read: Colossians 3:18-21

The most important relationship is one's relationship with God. Get that right through active faith in Christ, from that priority, all other relationships can be governed. When I perform marriage ceremonies, I always say to the couple: *If you will both maintain an active love for God, there is no issue or challenge you cannot face and work through together.*

In Colossians 3:18-21, Paul tells us how it should be, as God's plan is respected. "Wives, submit to your husbands, as is fitting in the Lord." This is not a vague submission that men can define to suit their interests or that women can dismiss or revise. This is submission "as is fitting in the Lord."

To learn more about how this should work, please consult Ephesians 5:22-33. There, you will discover that the husband's headship is controlled by such a high level of love; it is the love that Christ has for the church. Further, his headship is that which "nourishes and cherishes."

The wife submits to this nourishing, cherishing love for her head because of her ultimate Head, Christ (1 Cor. 11:3). Should any husband dogmatically define his headship in terms of any barking of commands to cater to his comfort, the next verse says: "do not be harsh with them!" If a man wants to read part of this passage, he needs to read all of it: "Do not be harsh with them."

When male headship and female submission are defined according to the words of the Lord in this text and in Ephesians 5, the relationship is "as fitting in the Lord." This requires, however, the love and respect of both husband and wife *for God*. Once that is their settled attitude about all of life, these instructions fall right into place and enable the partners to deal with the challenges of the relationship.

Children are part of the family, and they are assigned responsibility: "obey your parents." The reason is given: "This pleases the Lord."

Just try to imagine a teenager having a conversation with the Apostle Paul: *"Brother Paul, my parents are not very smart. In fact, I'm smarter than my parents. They have these old, outdated habits, rules, and tradi-*

tions. They just drive me crazy sometimes. They really don't understand me or give me what I want. What should I do, brother Paul?"

Do you think the answer would be any different today? "Children, obey your parents in everything, for this pleases the Lord."

An especially important word is given to fathers: "Do not provoke your children, lest they become discouraged."

There is a specific attitude or manner of dealing with children that can be tempting and habitual. The children disturb your peace, and your reaction is to yell at them or berate them. While children need a negative response to bad behavior, this verse warns against being insulting, offensive, and demeaning. Exaggerated, reactionary discipline has negative consequences, just as an absence of discipline has consequences. God teaches us a balanced approach in His Word. Take your family to church Sunday and worship God.

ANOTHER LOOK!

HUSBANDS

"Husbands, love your wives and do not be embittered against them" (Colossians 3:19 NASB 95). There should be no discussion among husbands about whether the Lord has instructed them regarding their duties and responsibilities in the home. Jesus has done that! Matthew begins his narrative about Joseph, Mary, and Jesus by letting us know about the good qualities Joseph possessed; even in a difficult situation, he was intent on doing the right thing (Matthew 1:18ff). Hebrews 13:4 says: "Marriage is to be held in honor among all, and the marriage bed is to be undefiled; for fornicators and adulterers God will judge." Our Lord emphasized the seriousness of joining oneself to another person; if a man cannot live faithfully with the wife of his youth, then maybe he shouldn't get married (Matthew 19:3-12).

The Apostle Peter, who was married, spoke about the sacred relationship between husband and wife. "You husbands in the same way, live with your wives in an understanding way, as with someone weaker, since she is a woman; and show her honor as a fellow heir of the grace of life, so that your prayers will not be hindered" (1 Peter 3:7). Sarah honored her husband, Abraham; wives today are to honor their husbands. One way they show honor is in submission. Submission to anyone, at any time, in any relationship raises red flags, starts fires, alienates couples, and makes people mad. Still, husbands have been given a leadership role in the home and family; wives must willingly submit to that leadership. Let us all recognize that any authority a husband has comes from the Lord (for submit see Ephesians 5:22; Colossians 3:18; 1 Peter 3:1; Titus 2:4). Husbands must not abdicate that position of leadership. Submission involves obedience for the husband and the wife. Unselfish exercise of leadership honors the Lord and helps the marriage—men, women, and children in the home benefit when family members do what they are supposed to do. The woman submits; this is fitting in the Lord. The husband leads because he is the head (authority; Greek = kephale).

Loving our wives as Christ loved the church will eliminate anger, resentment, and bitterness. Yes, some husbands are overbearing, harsh, and resentful toward their wives. Paul told husbands to love themselves; that is, there must be and generally is, an attitude of respect, care, and attention paid to one's own existence (Ephesians 5:28-29). Just so, in the exercise of loving headship, husbands think first of their wives, their needs, and their welfare.

Here is a sermon for preachers; these ideas are taken from *Colossians and Philemon, Baker Exegetical Commentary on the New Testament*, G. K. Beale, 313-315.

Believers Should Live Out the New-Creation Lifestyle in the Family
Colossians 3

A. We are new creatures in Christ 3:1-4
B. His death and resurrection make this possible 1:15-20
C. New creatures in Christ wear new clothes 3:5ff

THE CHRISTIAN WIFE

A. Submits to her husband; in doing so, she honors Christ
B. The honor and joy of motherhood; the family, children

THE CHRISTIAN HUSBAND

A. Loves his wife as Christ loves the church
B. Honors his wife; this honors Christ
C. Recognizes the emotional and physical makeup of his wife
D. Applies 1 Corinthians 13 every day

THE YOUNG PEOPLE IN THE HOME

A. Respect father and mother; this honors the Lord
B. Accepts teaching from parents as did Jesus
C. Lack of discipline results in heartache

Con: Husbands, wives, and children are analogues of Christ and the church; Love each other, Love the Lord, Love His church

Randy Harshbarger

DAY 17

Read: Colossians 3:22-4:1

Being a Christian isn't just about being forgiven and going to heaven (though both are obviously critical). Living as a Christian forms the basis of all your life. You are a Christian every day, wherever you are, in every relationship, in fair weather, and when the storms beat against you.

For instance, in New Testament times, there were Christians who were domestic servants or bondservants, making their living in a form of servitude. {This is not a good place to go into detail, but the servitude in places like Colossae was not like abusive pre-civil war slavery.}

Paul tells Christians who were bondservants to obey their earthly masters. Disobedience would (1) go against the general principle of cooperative agreement, submission, and work ethic, (2) could easily put the rebellious servant in danger, and (3) would not serve as good testimony for evangelism (see Philippians 1). {The stipulation given elsewhere in Scripture applies here. In any relationship of submission to another human being, if the superior requires something sinful, Christians must refuse. See Acts 5:29}.

As applied today to employee-employer relationships, observe carefully how specific this is: "in everything" the worker is to serve obediently. (Everything except—as noted above—the qualification derived from Acts 5:29).

"Not by way of eye-service, as people-pleasers, but with sincerity of heart, fearing the Lord."

This addresses a common experience of workers/employees appearing to be busy and productive when the supervisor or boss is around. (When the boss is away, the workers will play—not Christian workers.)

An absence of ethics in the workplace is not befitting those who have committed to serve the Lord. Our commitment is to "with sincerity" obey our superiors, "fearing the Lord."

Responsibility is also placed on "masters" or employers. The paragraph continues into the first verse of chapter four: "Masters, treat your bondservants justly and fairly, knowing that you also have a Master in heaven." God never places responsibility just on one side of a relationship. Just as workers are to seriously accept their duty, their superiors must also be just and fair, knowing they serve a higher Master. All of this is about and directed to the Highest Master.

Then, look back into the text and see how Paul takes this outside of the workplace to all of life: "Whatever you do, work heartily, as for the Lord and not for men, knowing that from the Lord you will receive the inheritance as your reward. You are serving the Lord Christ."

No matter where I am located, what my personal responsibilities are, who I am with, and all other such considerations— I am a servant of the Lord. All that I do should reflect this. And, if the Lord has promised a reward to me—I should take that awareness with me into every dimension of my existence.

Likewise, "the wrongdoer will be paid back for the wrong he has done, and there is no partiality." We may serve the Lord daily by desiring the good and resisting the wrong.

ANOTHER LOOK!

RELATIONSHIPS

"Slaves, in all things obey those who are your masters on earth, not with external service, as those who merely please men, but with sincerity of heart, fearing the Lord. Whatever you do, do your work heartily, as for the Lord rather than for men, knowing that from the Lord you will receive the reward of the inheritance. It is the Lord Christ whom you serve. For he who does wrong will receive the consequences of the wrong which he has done, and that without partiality. Masters, grant to your slaves justice and fairness, knowing that you too have a Master in heaven" (Colossians 3:22-4:1 NASB 95).

There are many relationships in God's word—husbands and wives, parents and children, citizens of world empires, citizens of God's kingdom, military men, merchants, and fishermen. This tells us that no one lives in total isolation. John Donne said: "No man is an island." The Apostle Paul said: "For not one of us lives for himself, and not one dies for himself" (Romans 14:7). In other words, Christianity involves everyday, practical issues of life. Our decisions and conduct as family members, citizens, workers, etc., must be motivated by the desire to please the Lord. The result of such a desire will be a good influence in the various walks of life. Even if you have a "forward master," you should still set a good example (1 Peter 2:18).

"Slavery in the Roman Empire was, like all historical systems of slavery, a process of domination" (*Paul and Politics*, Richard A. Horsely, ed., 110). Slavery was a social institution and a social relationship. The inner workings of slavery (do this, do that) were pragmatic; but more, slavery helped perpetuate a division between the higher and lower classes of society. If you could subjugate a slave, you elevated yourself in the eyes of your friends and society—a society that was built on domination.

Paul recognized that slavery existed. Consider 1 Corinthians 7:21-24. "Were you called while a slave? Do not worry about it; but if you are able also to become free, rather do that. For he who was called in the Lord while a slave, is the Lord's freedman; likewise, he who was called while free, is Christ's slave. You were bought with a price; do not become slaves of men. Brethren, each one is to remain with God in that condition in which he was called." Should a Christian who was a slave seek freedom (manumission)? Should that Christian remain in his present situation?

Whatever the answer, Paul says: Your relationship to Jesus is not affected either way; rejoice and don't worry about your present state.

While Paul was a Roman citizen, there is no suggestion that he was "upper crust." Some Christians owned slaves; even some slaves owned slaves. Owning slaves did not automatically mean you were going to prosper in any significant way. Paul said to the Colossians: Whether slave or free, your greatest responsibility is to the Lord. Work hard, treat others fairly, remember you are not the ultimate Master. He is watching over you. Paul might have said, and surely, he believed, that there just might be some slaves in heaven. "There is neither Jew nor Greek, there is neither slave nor free man, there is neither male nor female; for you are all one in Christ Jesus" (Galatians 3:28).

Randy Harshbarger

DAY 18

Read: Colossians 4:2-6

"Continue" is a significant word for Christians to highlight as the New Testament is read. Think of baptism as the beginning. Everything after that is *continuing*. And in this passage, prayer deserves that continued activity of faith. And in those prayers, we should watch to be certain thanksgiving is present. (Can you imagine thanking God too much?)

Paul expresses his interest in the prayers of Christians in Colossae. This is one of those several texts where the Holy Spirit gives us a window into the heart of Paul.

Consider all that Paul might have asked for. *Pray that we are safe, well-fed, adequately supported, received with amazing hospitality, and never criticized.*

Instead, Paul said, "pray also for us, that God may open to us a door for the word, to declare the mystery of Christ, on account of which I am in prison, that I may make it clear, which is how I ought to speak."

What emerges here is the apostle's priority: Preaching the Word! And do not miss how clear he is about being clear! He wanted to be so clear that people hearing him would understand the revelation of the "mystery of Christ." [This is not a mystery hidden but a mystery revealed; see Rom. 16:25-27.]

As Christians continue their walk with the Lord after baptism, they must "walk in wisdom toward outsiders." There is an ongoing relationship we have with non-Christians. We interact with neighbors, co-workers, and friends who are not committed to Christ. One part of our evangelistic outreach must be the testimony of our lives—the influence of our behavior and reactions. We are to be the light of the world.

Making the best use of the time, or in some translations, this is worded, "redeeming the time." Wouldn't it be great to log on to Amazon, navigate to the "time department," and buy some extra hours, days, or years?

Dream on. What God expects of His people is to wisely use the time He grants to us. We are charged in this passage to be good stewards of time. This involves the acceptance of the time the generous Creator gives us (with thanksgiving), then the use of that time with such devotion that we glorify Him and grow in our service to Christ.

Part of this good use of time is, "Let your speech always be gracious, seasoned with salt, so that you may know how you ought to answer each person."

Follow this carefully. If a generous Creator gives us time and all the other blessings we do not deserve, shouldn't we be gracious in all that we think and say? No doubt.

"Seasoned with salt" is not salty language in the crude sense. It is speech that comes from those who are the salt of the earth. It seasons and makes the various relationships and conversations we are part of pleasant and useful. The responsibility is to "know how you ought to answer each person." This is about thoughtful speech, not impulsive speech. Helpful, not hurtful. Spiritual, not carnal. Godly, not ungodly.

Continue in these things!

ANOTHER LOOK!

FINAL LESSONS

"Devote yourselves to prayer, keeping alert in it with an attitude of thanksgiving; praying at the same time for us as well, that God will open up to us a door for the word, so that we may speak forth the mystery of Christ, for which I have also been imprisoned; that I may make it clear in the way I ought to speak. Conduct yourselves with wisdom toward outsiders, making the most of the opportunity. Let your speech always be with grace, as though seasoned with salt, so that you will know how you should respond to each person" (Colossians 4:2-6 NASV 95).

Here are a few final lessons from Paul. These final thoughts help to shore up and solidify the faith and daily living of the Colossians. These admonitions are practical and doable; they will help us, too, as we walk with Jesus in faith.

1. We must not give up our faith; we must continue to persevere. We are alert spiritually. We weaken our spiritual defenses when we neglect to pray to God. Paul prayed for the Colossians; he needed their prayers.

2. We live with thanksgiving in our hearts; we are thankful for God, Jesus, heaven's grace, and the assurance that God loves us. In sorrow, thanksgiving, times of blessings, or times of peril, we can still be thankful.

3. We must seek open doors of opportunities to influence others with the Gospel. Paul was in prison because he preached the mystery of Christ; the fulfillment of God's eternal purpose in Christ was, and is, the message all need to hear. We must still think of our relationships to others, how we behave and why. The Colossians needed to work on being effective in their teaching of God's will.

4. We can pray for each other. Paul wanted his brethren to pray for him.

5. We must walk in wisdom, especially walking in consideration of the fact that those "outside" are watching. This is a key element in reaching the lost. Others may not listen to a sermon; they will, though, listen to the sermons we preach by our daily living. Wise living stems from faith in Christ and His will.

6. We must do God's will today! Buy up the opportunities; don't waste what precious time you have left.

7. Speech seasoned with salt can heal, sting, and preserve. Speech that is spiritually fresh and vital will bless and teach others.

Paul wanted the Colossians to shoulder their responsibilities for Christ. Teachers want to inculcate in their students the needed lessons that will help whatever their field of endeavor may be. Our steps in faith may be early steps; the Colossians were not saturated with the gospel. Paul, if he went to Colossae at all, couldn't have been there for a long period of time. It was unlikely that this veteran prisoner could ever return to see his brothers and sisters one more time. He loves them, is thankful for them, has tried to help them, and now, he wants to give one last brief message of encouragement. Thank you, Paul. Thank you, Lord.

Randy Harshbarger

DAY 19

Read: Colossians 4:7-18

These final greetings afford us an intriguing insight into Paul, the human being who was a servant of Christ. If your picture of Paul is something like a traveling lecturer who shows up to deliver his speech, then moves on to the next appointment; a lonely, isolated soul—passages like this destroy that image.

Paul was engaged with people. He loved God and loved God's people. He poured out his heart about his affection and appreciation for good people. It has also been observed this reads a little like an address book or contact list (similar to Romans 16).

If Paul had had email and texting, I don't have any doubt he would use those methods to communicate with people. Paul@HolySpirit.com, someone once suggested.

Tychicus knew enough about Paul to tell others about his "activities." Paul considered him as a "beloved brother." Onesimus was also held in high regard by Paul: "our faithful and beloved brother." These two men would tell the Colossian Christians about Paul's work.

Aristarchus was a "fellow prisoner" who sent his greetings. Mark, the cousin of Barnabus, kept Paul in good company, along with Justus. Another servant of Christ in this close network was Epaphras. He was one of the Colossian group, who prayed fervently for the saints. He was a hard worker. Luke is included, "the beloved physician," and at the time of this writing, Demas is mentioned among the faithful.

Note From Matthew Henry

> Paul had differed with Barnabas, on the account of this Mark, yet he is not only reconciled, but recommends him to the churches; an example of a truly Christian and forgiving spirit. If men have been guilty of a fault, it must not always be remembered against them. We must forget as well as forgive. The apostle had comfort in the communion of saints and ministers. One is his fellow-ser-

vant, another his fellow-prisoner, and all his fellow-workers, working out their own salvation, and endeavouring to promote the salvation of others. The effectual, fervent prayer is the prevailing prayer, and availeth much. The smiles, flatteries, or frowns of the world, the spirit of error, or the working of self-love, leads many to a way of preaching and living which comes far short of fulfilling their ministry. But those who preach the same doctrine as Paul, and follow his example, may expect the Divine favour and blessing.[1]

This warm exchange included "the brothers at Laodicea and to Nympha and the church in her house."

> *"And when this letter has been read among you, have it also read in the church of the Laodiceans, and see that you also read the letter from Laodicea."*

This is important. It reflects the interest of the Holy Spirit that inspired writings be circulated and read (see Eph. 3:1-4). These epistles were not private. Rather, they were intended for public access and future circulation.

"And say to Archippus, 'See that you fulfill the ministry that you have received in the Lord.'"

Then, "I, Paul, write this greeting with my own hand. Remember my chains. Grace be with you."

---

[1] Henry, M., & Scott, T. (1997). *Matthew Henry's Concise Commentary* (Col. 4:10). Oak Harbor, WA: Logos Research Systems.

ANOTHER LOOK!

WHERE SHOULD WE ASSEMBLE?

Colossians 4:15: "Greet the brethren who are in Laodicea and also Nympha and the church that is in her house" (NASB 95).

Every so often, a spate of sermons, articles, and books emerge, extolling the value of "house churches." The basic premise is that New Testament Christians met in houses, the result being, a "house church." Explicitly or implicitly, the message is: If you do not meet in a house, you are not a New Testament church. Yes, Christians did meet in houses or homes owned or occupied by someone, probably a fellow believer. Yet, the house church movement goes far beyond simply the need for finding a place to meet. Christ's will determines who His people (His church) are. There is no intrinsic value in a particular building of any kind, whether a house, rented hall, brand new church building, or, as in New Testament times, the temple. Early Christians sometimes met in the temple courtyards, a convenient place to gather, given the size of these early groups. If you are going to insist on assembling in the temple courtyard, where is the temple? Where is the courtyard? Consider this good summary from brother Jim Deason: "The truth is that early churches did not meet only in houses. They also met in the temple (Acts 2:46), by a riverside (Acts 16:13), in the school of Tyrannus (Acts 19:9), and in a synagogue-type place (Jas. 2:2). There is no exclusive pattern regarding the place where Christians of the first century met. Expedience determined where they assembled" (*True Worship*: Florida College Annual Lectures, 2005, Florida College Bookstore, 2005, Jim Deason, 172).

Yes, house churches existed in the first century. Studying Colossians includes some discussion about the church in that city. Paul mentions several names in chapter four and several in his letter to Philemon; did the church meet in Philemon's house? He would have had the means to house a group of Christians on Sundays or at other times (for the wealthy providing places to meet for those without means, see *The Moral World of the First Christians*, Westminster Press, 1986, Wayne Meeks, 120; for connection of Colossians to Philemon see, *Relationships in the Messianic Time: A Commentary on Philemon*, Deward Publishing, David McClister, 25-29). Surmising can go in either direction.

Meet in a house, in a building, or under a tree. When you meet, do what the Lord says to do. Christians who seek to do "everything" in the name of the Lord will work hard to ensure their family relationships are in line with Christ. Meet in a house, in a building, or under a tree. Just do His will.

Randy Harshbarger

DAY 20

BOOKENDS

Unlike Paul's letter to the Philippians, there seems to be little indication in his letter to the Colossians that he anticipated a release from prison. Tychicus is on his way to Colossae, carrying Paul's letter to the "saints and faithful brethren in Christ." His letter was short but powerful; he dealt blow after blow against the false, pseudo teachings from those who challenged the power and supremacy of Christ. We can only imagine Paul's feelings as he sends Onesimus back home to Philemon.

Onesimus, once a slave of man, is now a slave of Christ. But Paul is not alone. Aristarchus, Mark, Jesus called Justus, and Epaphras were on hand to bolster his faith; these men were true yokefellows with their beloved mentor and friend.

Paul's letter closes with a personal salutation. Can we imagine the difficulty of raising manacled hands one last time to write these parting words? His salutation was not a plea for sympathy. Rather, Paul asserts his authority as an apostle of Christ. What he wrote was true and inspired; it came from the Lord. So, listen!

Paul was in chains. Chains hardly resonate with our lives of abundance, protection, and self-sufficiency. Paul is not asking for sympathy; he was in prison for the benefit of others. Do we find our motivation in his chains, his bonds, his imprisonments?

Was Paul the apostle to the Gentiles? Did he ever preach to the Jews? Was he strong and forceful regardless of his audience? Yes, yes, and yes! Notice, though, how Paul began and ended his letter to the Colossians. "To the saints and faithful brethren in Christ who are at Colossae: Grace to you and peace from God our Father" (Colossians 1:2 NASB 95). "Paul, write this greeting with my own hand. Remember my imprisonment. Grace be with you" (Colossians 4:18). If you and I are going to have a good beginning and a good end, let the bookends of our lives be God's grace.

Randy Harshbarger

www.ingramcontent.com/pod-product-compliance
Lightning Source LLC
LaVergne TN
LVHW020938090426
835512LV00020B/3409